LIVING
WEST

LIVING WEST

NEW RESIDENTIAL ARCHITECTURE IN SOUTHERN CALIFORNIA

SAM LUBELL

THE MONACELLI PRESS

Thanks to all the architects and photographers involved for their ingenious work and their patient cooperation. Thanks also to Stacee Lawrence for her good nature and intelligent guidance, to Andrea Monfried and Gianfranco Monacelli for again encouraging my work, to Elizabeth White for taking such care with the production, to Penny Hardy and Elizabeth Oh for their beautiful design and to my family and Carri for supporting me, inspiring me, and loving me.

INTRODUCTION 8

ON CLIFF'S EDGE

BELZBERG ARCHITECTS SKYLINE RESIDENCE LOS ANGELES 2008 / 14

JOHNSTON MARKLEE HILL HOUSE PACIFIC PALISADES 2004 / 22

CALLAS SHORTRIDGE ARCHITECTS ROCHMAN HOUSE LOS ANGELES 2000 / 28

PREDOCK FRANE ARCHITECTS TWIN HOUSES PACIFIC PALISADES 2008 / 34

ESCHER GUNEWARDENA ARCHITECTURE JAMIE HOUSE PASADENA 2000 / 42

SAFDIE RABINES ARCHITECTS TREE HOUSE SAN DIEGO 2000 / 46

URBAN INNOVATIONS

XTEN ARCHITECTURE SURFHOUSE HERMOSA BEACH 2007 / 52

JOHN FRIEDMAN ALICE KIMM KING RESIDENCE SANTA MONICA 2008 / 58

STEFFEN LEISNER/SYNTAX 1+3=1 HOUSE VENICE 2006 / 64

LLOYD RUSSELL R3 TRIANGLE BUILDING SAN DIEGO 2006 / 70

TOURAINE RICHMOND ARCHITECTS ONE-WINDOW HOUSE VENICE 2005 / 74

MICHELE SAEE LINNIE HOUSE VENICE 2005 / 78

RADICAL TRANSFORMATIONS

TECHENTIN BUCKINGHAM ARCHITECTURE LOS FELIZ RESIDENCE LOS ANGELES 2008 / 86

DALY GENIK 823 PALMS VENICE 2009 / 94

STUDIO PALI FEKETE ARCHITECTS BEUTH RESIDENCE WEST HOLLYWOOD 2005 / 100

TIGHE ARCHITECTURE TIGERTAIL BRENTWOOD 2007 / 108

STEVEN LOMBARDI 330 NEPTUNE ENCINITAS 2008 / 114

NEIL M. DENARI ARCHITECTS ALAN-VOO HOUSE CULVER CITY 2007 / 120

OPEN AND AIRY

ABRAMSON TEIGER ARCHITECTS KELLY HOUSE BRENTWOOD 2006 / 128

GRIFFIN ENRIGHT ARCHITECTS POINT DUME RESIDENCE MALIBU 2007 / 136

BARBARA BESTOR ARCHITECTURE MARCO PLACE VENICE 2009 / 146

STEVEN EHRLICH 700 PALMS RESIDENCE VENICE 2005 / 152

JONATHAN SEGAL LEMPERLE RESIDENCE LA JOLLA 2008 / 160

ENVIRONMENTALLY MINDED

SANDER ARCHITECTS RESIDENCE FOR A BRIARD CULVER CITY 2008 / 168

OFFICE OF MOBILE DESIGN SEATRAIN LOS ANGELES 2003 / 174

PUGH + SCARPA ARCHITECTS SOLAR UMBRELLA HOUSE VENICE 2005 / 182

TAALMAN KOCH ARCHITECTURE OFF-GRID ITHOUSE PIONEERTOWN 2007 / 188

MOUNTAINSIDE RETREATS

AGPS.ARCHITECTURE TOPANGA RANCH TOPANGA CANYON 2004 / 196

LORCAN O'HERLIHY ARCHITECTS JAI HOUSE CALABASAS 2004 / 204

OLSON SUNDBERG KUNDIG ALLEN ARCHITECTS MONTECITO RESIDENCE MONTECITO 2008 / 212

KANNER ARCHITECTS MALIBU 5 MALIBU 2006 / 222

ALEKS ISTANBULLU ARCHITECTS LAGO VISTA BEVERLY HILLS 2007 / 230

PHOTOGRAPHY CREDITS 238

INTRODUCTION SAM LUBELL

ABOVE Wallace Cunningham, Crescent House | RIGHT Ray Kappe, LivingHome

LOOK ACROSS A HILLSIDE IN SOUTHERN CALIFORNIA and you will see an unbelievable variety of residential styles, types, forms, and volumes. Traditional Mission-style haciendas mingle with sleek midcentury modern residences, tiny ranch houses, nondescript tract homes, huge McMansions, Victorians, ramshackle beach houses, and Arts and Crafts bungalows. In short, one of the most varied urban fabrics in the United States, if not the world.

To many this jumble represents freedom. Freedom from established, accepted aesthetics, from space limitations found in denser cities, and from harsh climates that limit a house's form and how it can interact with its surroundings. That freedom, combined with enlightened clients and a love for the single-family house, has made Southern California a center for residential innovation and experimentation for over a century. Millions of people have come to this beautiful stretch of land to start anew, and talented architects have been no exception.

From Frank Lloyd Wright, Rudolph Schindler, Richard Neutra, Charles and Ray Eames, John Lautner, and Pierre Koenig to Frank Gehry and Richard Meier, successive generations of experimental architects working in Southern California have continued to rethink contemporary conventions. They have broken the barriers that separate inside from outside, rethought how rooms and people should interact, and used inexpensive materials to create new building methods and styles. This tradition thrives even as new Southern California designers face challenges including a reduction in open land and ever more strict zoning regulations. Veteran firms as well as hungry young designers both prosper here. While influenced by the designs of their predecessors, they are adapting to—and are stimulated by—restrictions that force creative solutions. Innovative forms, plans, programs, and techniques continue to emerge regularly.

Perhaps above all, architects working in Southern California cannot be accused of being timid. They exploit new technologies to create innovative forms and structures, and to build in locations that were once deemed impossible. Striking examples include Escher GuneWardena's Jamie Residence in Pasadena, a rectangular structure lofted high in the air like a bridge to provide breathtaking views and minimize disruption of the land underneath, Patrick Tighe's Tigertail, with its angular, cantilevered second-floor roof shaped like an airplane wing, and Johnston Marklee's Hill House, with its seamless envelope and precarious site on the side of a steep ravine. Others, like Wallace Cunningham's Crescent House with its multiple ramps, terraces, and curving concrete forms, are as much sculpture as house.

These new structures, like the classic designs that came before them, are designed to embrace the varied, beautiful landscapes and benign climate of the area, just in different ways. Sliding glass doors, windows, and skylights continue to increase in size and in their ability to cleverly disappear discreetly into walls, opening structures fully to the outside. Houses today often meld unobtrusively into their surroundings, adopting the colors,

ABOVE SH Architecture, Abbot Kinney Residence | CENTER De Maria Design, Redondo Beach House
RIGHT Assembledge+, Ridgewood Residence

textures, and even topography of the land they rest upon—Griffin Enright's Point Dume residence curves sinuously in response to its lot's natural undulations; its cladding and interior fittings were also chosen to match the surrounding hardscape. Safdie Rabines's aptly named Tree House in San Diego is perched on the edge of a heavily wooded ravine and thanks to outsized sliding doors and clerestory windows opens so completely that birds fly through it as if it were part of the forest itself.

A wide variety of sustainable materials and prefabrication techniques are incorporated to adapt new construction to today's acute environmental and economic pressures. The vast majority of houses in this book can be considered "green" to various degrees and often feature solar panels, radiant heating, gray water treatment, recycled materials, and carefully designed passive ventilation and cooling. Some, like the Solar Umbrella House by Pugh + Scarpa, derive their entire form from sustainable elements, in this case eighty-nine solar panels used as a canopy that shapes the roof and one facade. The Office of Mobile Design rearranged a suite of found shipping containers in an abandoned lot near downtown L.A. to create one of the most unique and livable structures in the region. De Maria Design's Redondo Beach House is also formed of shipping containers, a perfect material for its oceanside location, since the corrugated metal is mold- and termite-resistant, not to mention cheap. Whitney Sander combined a prefabricated shell with custom interior materials and recycled components like insulation made of shredded blue jeans and pressed sunflower-seed boards to create a "hybrid" house large enough to host classical music concerts in, and for only $130 per square foot. Star architects have also joined the sustainable home design movement. Ray Kappe, for example, offers warm, intricate, light-infused prefab structures that can be configured in numerous ways—to suit individual sites—through the LivingHomes company.

Continuing the theme of reducing and reusing materials, firms are also shaping radical new architecture by reconfiguring existing homes. After all, there's nothing greener than building with what's already there. Techentin Buckingham architects transformed an unremarkable 1950s tract home in the Los Feliz neighborhood of L.A. into a fresh, original amalgam of old and new by adding a textural wooden rainscreen, irregularly placed windows with cheerful colored frames, and by reconfiguring the formerly cramped interior layout to suit a contemporary family lifestyle. Daly Genik similarly wrapped a 1980s bungalow and detached garage in a new exterior surface, this time a folding, perforated gray steel screen that completely changes its sedate character, limits solar gain, and increases privacy. Carefully crafted small additions, such as Aleks Istanbullu's jewellike Lago Vista library and guest house and Neil M. Denari's ultramodern, colorful extension to a plain stucco house not only enlarge existing structures, but infuse them with a completely new personality.

In response to an ever-shrinking buildable area, architects are also designing homes in more and more difficult and restrictive environments—and that doesn't just include the

ABOVE LEFT Cigolle X Coleman, TR+2 StudioHouse | CENTER Standard, Tree House
RIGHT Macy Architecture, Sustainable Steel Home

sides of cliffs and canyons. Agps.architecture and Olson Sundberg Kundig Allen both built recently in the middle of known fire zones. Thick steel envelopes and careful landscaping minimize the risk to the structures should a wildfire approach, but cannot remove it completely. Other firms wedge inventive envelopes into tight urban neighborhoods. In these cases, the designers either make the decision to open up the house to embrace and celebrate the streetscape, or find creative ways—deep light wells, interior courtyards, even placing public and private spaces in separate buildings—to create secluded oases.

The architecture of today's Southern California houses is often warmer and more diverse in its use of materials than that of its modernist predecessors as well. Many designers in these pages incorporate timber cladding or textured metals like copper and Cor-Ten steel. Custom elements are also often featured, and add individuality, rawness, and even coziness. Lloyd Russell, for example, clad much of his R3 Triangle Building in San Diego in concrete shaped into rough, uneven blocks, a touch of texture and individuality for an already unusual building wedged into an ultra-tight lot. Michele Saee clad his Linnie House with a combination of angled plywood and concrete that appears to burst out of the building's envelope. Belzberg Architects used many inexpensive, off-the-shelf materials to create elegant, folded forms. Others have looked for inspiration and practicality to new materials like Styrofoam, Sarnafil, polycarbonate, fiberglass, Grailcoat, and Trespa panels.

Like much architecture today, these houses defy being classified into one specific style—they cater to specific conditions rather than a school of thought. Perhaps extreme customization to landscape, light, and topography, guided by these architects' artistic visions and technological capabilities, is today's style. Most new construction in this area, however, still falls into the category of mundane developers' models, and while a few pockets like Venice and Pacific Palisades have planners that are receptive to innovation, other planning departments in the area can be quite conservative. Approvals for many of the unorthodox homes in this book took years, but it is encouraging that the push persists.

Challenges increase as the area becomes more crowded and open lots disappear. But architects will persevere, fitting new houses tightly into infill sites and helping to create a sense of community that many here crave. Tight spaces come with challenges, but also bring new contexts and settings that promote creativity.

Architectural innovation in Southern California can be seen in commercial and multi-family housing, but more prevalently in single-family housing. Architects continue coming here from around the world to experiment—not with careless abandon, but with an adventurous and serious investigation of tectonics, space, form, and material. Thanks to changing circumstances and a constant output of fresh ideas, Southern California has once again become known for its striking, thought-provoking residential architecture. These recent houses refuse to adhere to rules established elsewhere, and for this the rest of the world continues to turn to them for inspiration.

ON CLIFF'S EDGE

BELZBERG ARCHITECTS SKYLINE RESIDENCE
LOS ANGELES 2008

1 GUEST HOUSE AND CARPORT | 2 DRIVE | 3 GRAVEL DECK | 4 LIVING /DINING | 5 INFINITY POOL | 6 BEDROOM | 7 MASTER BEDROOM

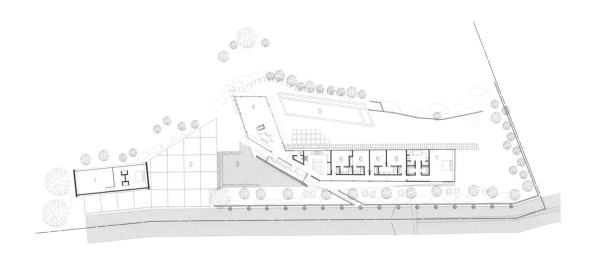

ABOVE A side of the guest house makes a perfect movie screen for viewers in the courtyard.

OPPOSITE Glass walls and doors on three sides of the living room afford spectacular vistas of the surrounding canyons and valley and provide access to the cliffside infinity pool.

IT TOOK ARCHITECT HAGY BELZBERG two years and several public meetings to convince officials at the Mulholland Scenic Corridor to allow him to construct this house on top of a thin ridgeline in Laurel Canyon. The residence exploits sweeping views of Los Angeles, the San Fernando Valley, and the Pacific Ocean, and harnesses the site's strong breezes and plentiful light. A large concrete armature controls these elements to keep the interior environment comfortable. The folded form and a wind-permeable screen—made of long, thin, pressure-treated wood panels with a translucent fiberglass screen behind it—prevent the sun's most intense rays from penetrating the living spaces.

The bent surface shapes both the main structure and a two-story guest house across the driveway. Young architects at Belzberg's firm formed the construction crew. Inexpensive, locally produced, low-tech materials such as storefront windows and off-the-shelf parts kept costs and transportation emissions to a minimum, making these structures as carbon neutral as possible.

The carefully positioned living room, which has floor-to-ceiling fritted glass on three sides and looks down on the rocky canyons below, does not receive any direct sunlight, just a warming glow. Neither does the open kitchen or entertainment room, for similar reasons of careful siting and shading. A row of sliding glass doors along the house's western facade overlooks a thin yard that contains a narrow pool edged up against a steep drop. Bedrooms also look out on this landscape, and their generous glass doors give the residents the ability to walk outside at any moment.

TOP Thin, angular concrete veils the house from intense sun and strong breezes while still allowing some of each to penetrate.
ABOVE Boundaries between the outside and inside are minimized along one side of each bedroom space.
OPPOSITE A geometric opening in the main screen frames a view.

Pivoting glass doors open to allow cool breezes to enter; spare furnishings and continuous glazing keep the focus on the stunning view.

JOHNSTON MARKLEE HILL HOUSE

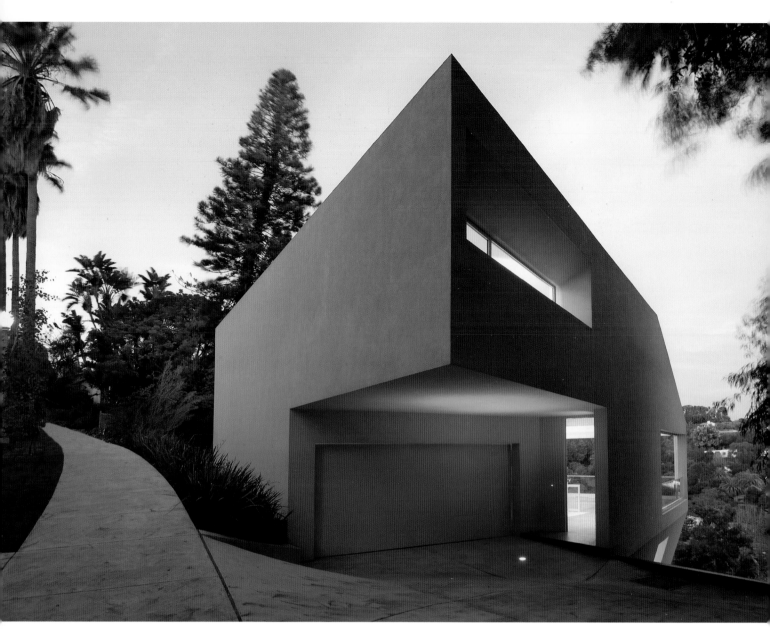

1 SUN ROOM | 2 MASTER BEDROOM | 3 CLOSET | 4 BATHROOM | 5 ENTRY | 6 LIVING ROOM | 7 DINING ROOM | 8 KITCHEN
9 GARAGE | 10 BEDROOM | 11 OFFICE

FIRST FLOOR

SECOND FLOOR

THIRD FLOOR

ABOUT A double-height living space seamlessly connects the house's top two levels.

OPPOSITE Solid forms on the streetside facade contrast with the glazing of the canyonside facade.

DESIGNING A HOUSE on an irregularly shaped lot on a steep, uneven slope overlooking Santa Monica Canyon was a tricky venture. To adapt to the topographical restrictions of the site, the architects designed this innovative form that erases the usual distinctions between roof and wall, interior and exterior.

Resembling a box with sides and corners that have been bent and folded in all directions, the house's contorted shape was modeled to hug the steep embankment and to fit into the area's strict height restrictions. The construction process wasn't easy: architects Sharon Johnston and Mark Lee oversaw a team that poured a concrete base and drilled deep caissons while, at times, hanging from trees on the side of the ravine. The house's facade is wrapped in a purplish-gray material called GrailCoat. Its elasticity allowed the structure to maintain this singular shape without any expansion joints or other visual interruptions.

The open plan of this minimally decorated, white residence flows effortlessly between three levels joined by a hanging stair. Its folded steel plates add a new set of sculptural geometries to the space. No windows face the street—views are focused on the deep canyon visible through 9-foot-tall, floor-to-ceiling sliding glass doors and strategically placed skylights that, due to the slanted roof, act as windows for the upper level. Standing in the double-height living room, which projects over the canyon thanks to the house's lunging envelope, feels like being perched in a nest. Breezes and the sounds of rustling leaves waft through the entire house. Birds do, in fact, occasionally fly straight through. The simple, lofted top floor containing a guest bedroom and office spies on this scene from above, while the lower-level master bedroom suite set into the hillside has a cozy ambience with its low ceilings, thick carpeting, and smaller, more deeply set windows. Steps leading from this lower level provide direct access to the canyon.

TOP The roof's shallow angle adds an intimate feeling to the otherwise open space.
ABOVE Long, linear glass doors slide completely open to frame the view and create
a sensation of being perched among the canyon's trees. | LEFT Glass railings, skylights,
an open stair, and an open plan work together to bring light deep into the house.

1 ENTRY HALL | 2 OFFICE | 3 LIVING/DINING | 4 DECK | 5 DEN | 6 GUEST BEDROOM | 7 GARAGE | 8 MASTER BEDROOM
9 GYM | 10 UTILITY ROOM

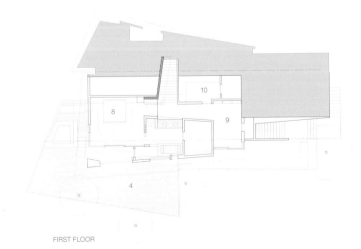

FIRST FLOOR

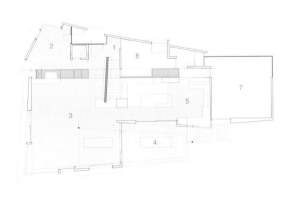

SECOND FLOOR

ABOVE Wooden beams that shade the exterior deck continue through to the dining room; walls tilt out toward the ocean, expanding interior square footage.

OPPOSITE An angled wood wall echoes the shape of the exterior while warming the interior.

SITED ON THE EDGE OF A MAJESTIC BLUFF, this house is barely noticeable from street level, where only glimpses of a simple, single-story gray bar are visible behind large hedges. A daring, sophisticated design that uses simple techniques to heighten a breathtaking view emerges only as the structure is approached.

The house's oceanfront facade angles outward, separating the main entrance from an office that the owners, who are psychiatrists, use with patients. This facade also features a zinc-clad garage and front door, surprisingly bold materials that provide a clue to the edgy overall design. The angular aesthetic continues on the far side of the house, where walls tilt out and in, with folds that mimic the stucco-clad structure's cliffside surroundings.

In the open-plan kitchen, dining, and living room space, long, narrow windows without corner joints carefully frame captivating views of a wide expanse of the Pacific Ocean. The continuous stretch of windows creates a strong sense of continuity between the indoors and outdoors, as does a long wooden pergola that covers both an outside deck and the interior dining room. Canted interior walls are used throughout the structure to shelter private spaces, such as bedrooms, from public view. Similarly, a canted exterior wall reaches out toward the ocean, giving the impression of increased square footage.

Several decks extend into the landscape, taking advantage of this promontory that affords some of the most panoramic views of any area on the coast. The lower level is surrounded by a wooden patio that is alternately narrow, wide, and inclined. The owners have the enviable quandary of deciding which to use on any given day.

ABOVE Posts and railings on the upper-level deck continue the theme of angled supports in use throughout the house.
OPPOSITE, ABOVE Windows without corner joints allow uninterrupted views to the horizon. | OPPOSITE, BELOW A unique shower shares panoramic views with the lower-level deck.

PREDOCK FRANE ARCHITECTS TWIN HOUSES

PACIFIC PALISADES 2008

1 BEDROOM | 2 FAMILY ROOM | 3 STORAGE | 4 LIGHT COURT | 5 UTILITY | 6 LIVING/DINING/KITCHEN | 7 COURTYARD | 8 DEN
9 GARAGE | 10 STUDY | 11 MASTER BEDROOM | 12 DECK

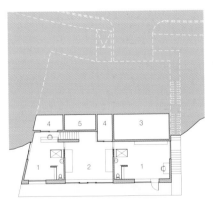

FIRST FLOOR

SECOND FLOOR

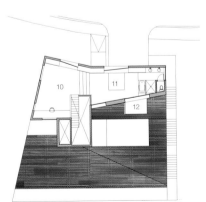

THIRD FLOOR

ABOVE Irregularly placed windows carved into the otherwise straightforward facade hint at the interior's unique geometry.

OPPOSITE Long lines on the smooth, dark redwood rainscreen create a sense of momentum and draw attention to the house's angular construction.

AS THEIR NAME SUGGESTS, these neighboring houses are basically identical. Their site is located in an area subject to the strict zoning ordinances of both Los Angeles and Pacific Palisades, spurring the architects to develop angular envelopes and distinctive but unobtrusive dark redwood facades that meet the restrictions while allowing the structures to fit elegantly into the neighborhood.

The side-by-side, stepped structures make their way down a steep ridge that leads into a densely forested canyon. Both of the three-story house designs, says architect Hadrian Predock, are a combination of modernist hillside architecture—meant, above all, to capture expansive views—and of more traditional courtyard forms intended to create private spaces and promote an intimate interaction with the environment. Sliding glass doors line much of the canyonside facade, including most of the 60-foot-long second floors that contain living rooms, dining rooms, and kitchens. Internal courtyards, placed between the living spaces and the hillside itself, offer secluded outdoor space and bounce light deep into the interior.

Both houses are designed so that all floors receive plentiful natural light. Topmost floors and courtyards receive light directly from above, while lower floors jut far out into the canyon to harvest rays. Bedrooms and studies, located on the upper levels, take advantage of the panoramic views, and a small canyonside porch provides outdoor space for these floors. Guest rooms and dens are on the bottom floors, and are nestled in thick, surrounding vegetation, making them feel like part of an entirely different, tropical landscape.

ABOVE Skylights and light courts bring the sun into all three floors of each building.
OPPOSITE A central stairwell is lit by asymmetric windows and light reflected from above.

Glass doors open the living/dining space to an interior courtyard on one side and the steep hillside's thick vegetation on the other.

ESCHER GUNEWARDENA ARCHITECTURE JAMIE HOUSE

PASADENA 2000

ESCHER GUNEWARDENA ARCHITECTURE JAMIE HOUSE

PASADENA 2000

1 ENTRY | 2 STUDY | 3 MASTER BEDROOM | 4 CLOSETS | 5 LIVING/DINING | 6 BALCONY | 7 FAMILY ROOM | 8 LAUNDRY
9 BEDROOM | 10 GARAGE

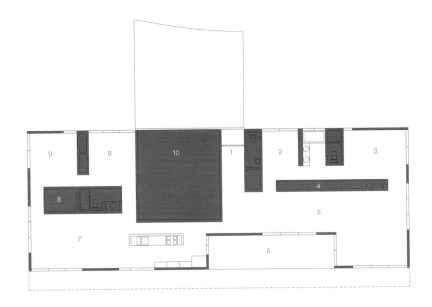

ABOVE Public spaces connect seamlessly with each other and with the view outside.

OPPOSITE Floor-to-ceiling windows make a mural of the valley.

THIS HOUSE IS CONSTRUCTED as if it were a bridge instead. The long, rectangular, wood-framed structure is lofted high on two 84-foot-long steel beams that rest on two concrete towers stabilized with deep caissons. This maneuver was designed to provide occupants with sweeping views of Pasadena, the Rose Bowl, and the entire San Gabriel Valley. The design also minimizes impact on the surrounding environment, since the landscape continues uninterrupted underneath—only 2 percent of the floor plate makes contact with the ground.

The 2,200-square-foot house, clad in a simple gridded cement board panel system, features open, connected public spaces—a white living room, kitchen, and den warmed with blond wood floors—and floor-to-ceiling windows that continue almost uninterrupted along its valley-side facade. A protruding deck with a sun visor that shades the space during the day but allows for stargazing at night, provides subtle spatial variation in an otherwise uniform public zone. In the rear of the house, sliding doors separate bedrooms and bathrooms, creating cozy retreats.

It took the firm more than two years to convince worried neighbors that the minimalist project would not detract from the area's scenery or appear out of place with the prevailing architectural style. Originally, explains architect Frank Escher, residents objected to its rawness and called for construction of a "skirt" under the house's freestanding base to cover its exposed underside.

SAFDIE RABINES ARCHITECTS TREE HOUSE
SAN DIEGO 2000

1 BEDROOM | 2 BALCONY | 3 BIRDCAGE | 4 LIVING ROOM | 5 DINING ROOM | 6 DECK

FIRST FLOOR

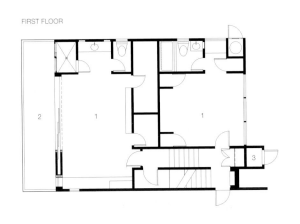

SECOND FLOOR

CONCEALED WELL IN THE STEEP, thickly wooded Goldfinch Canyon in San Diego's Mission Hills neighborhood, this project is not technically a tree house, but it does feel like one. The three-level, steel-framed, timber-clad structure does not rest tenuously on any actual branches, although it projects far into the forested canyon, embedded firmly into the earth on one end and hovering on columns on the other. It embraces its surroundings to such an extent that, at times, it becomes difficult to distinguish inside from out, particularly when the large windows and doors are fully open. A large birdcage for the family's pet parrot was built directly into the rear of the structure, affording him leafy views.

The 1,400-square-foot house consists of four main, interconnected zones, each on a different plane: living room, kitchen, master bedroom, and rooftop deck. Each story is exposed to the canyon, and a dense cover of eucalyptus filters the sunlight, keeping the house naturally cool. This constant connection to the elements and an open plan make the rooms in this moderately sized house feel spacious. The most airy of these is the double-height living room, featuring sliding doors along three of its four walls. A large bank of clerestory windows provides the adjacent kitchen—on a split level, constructed to accommodate the slope of the hill underneath—with views both out and up. The bedroom, on the bottom floor, is much smaller and feels appropriately cozy. Stairs are arranged to one side to minimize the square footage allotted to circulation, and move outdoors for rooftop access.

URBAN INNOVATIONS

XTEN ARCHITECTURE SURFHOUSE
HERMOSA BEACH 2007

1 BEDROOM | 2 GARAGE | 3 KITCHEN/DINING | 4 LIVING | 5 TERRACE

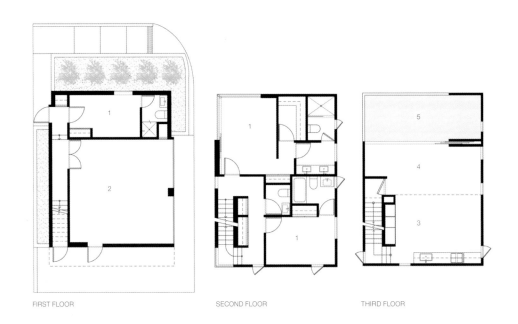

FIRST FLOOR   SECOND FLOOR   THIRD FLOOR

ABOVE Due to its overhang, the deck serves as an outdoor room and an airy extension of the top floor living space.

OPPOSITE Floor-to-ceiling windows allow plenty of California sunlight to penetrate a bedroom.

OVERLEAF The extended balcony frames splendid views of the neighborhood and ocean.

IN A NEIGHBORHOOD FULL of faux Spanish villas and ramshackle beach houses, this contemporary dwelling does not fit particularly well—and that's a good thing. Compared with its alternately ornate or dilapidated neighbors, the compact three-story structure appears serenely monolithic: a single box darkly clad in shiplapped rough cedar intended to wear over time and relate the house to its natural environment. The virtually seamless dark exterior and irregularly placed windows obscure the viewer's ability to differentiate individual floors. The exterior color contrasts dramatically with other residences in the vicinity, as well as with its own very light, airy interiors of white walls and bamboo floors.

The notable fissure in the street-side facade's top floor is a large, angular section carved out to form a balcony that provides views to the ocean without sacrificing privacy or shade. Sliding panels that disappear into walls allow the kitchen and living room to open onto the balcony, essentially making one extensive, outdoor room of them all. Panoramas from this level are eclipsed only by those taken in from the house's small rooftop deck. The rest of the 1,400-square-foot house consists of a vertical progression of rooms. The entry floor comprises a guest room and office in front and a garage at the rear. The second floor includes a master bedroom suite in front and a second bedroom that cantilevers over the garage below to maximize interior space for a growing family in a strictly zoned urban setting.

JOHN FRIEDMAN ALICE KIMM KING RESIDENCE
SANTA MONICA 2008

1 FOYER | 2 OFFICE | 3 WINE CELLAR | 4 LIVING/DINING | 5 KITCHEN | 6 DINING ROOM | 7 DEN | 8 GARAGE | 9 TERRACE
10 BEDROOM | 11 MASTER BEDROOM

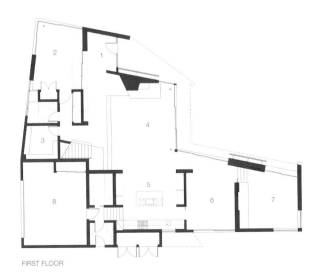

FIRST FLOOR

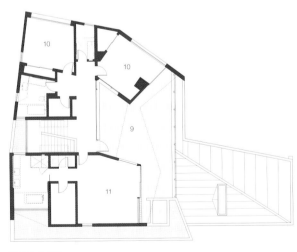

SECOND FLOOR

ABOVE The firm designed built-in timber cabinetry that echoes the facade's sense of movement.

OPPOSITE The house's inter-connected, folding planes simultaneously open the home and provide privacy.

THE SANTA MONICA COUPLE that built this house needed to make a good impression. They had torn down the ranch house of one of their street's long-time former residents to make way for this much more modern structure, so they thought that choosing an open design would make it easier to befriend the neighbors. The couple commissioned architects John Friedman and Alice Kimm to build a two-story structure that invitingly unwraps itself to the street. A series of continuous folded planes make their way around an exposed core, enclosing its residents in relative privacy while providing open views of the neighborhood and symbolically embracing the area. They also pushed the house away from the street to make room for a large front yard that slopes gently away from the front facade, providing a second-floor view that stretches all the way to the ocean.

Opening the house provided other perks as well: light pours in through the central exposure, the lovely neighborhood becomes the focal point for all views, and the folded planes break down the mass of the fairly large building. The decorative scheme on the exterior walls also breaks radically from the neighborhood's prevailing architectural style. Its pattern of alternating horizontal bands of yellow and white—offset with smaller walls made of thin, vertical, dark wood planks—gives the house texture, a visual rhythm, and echoes colors selected for the garden by the wife, who is studying to become a landscape architect.

The interior's lofty ceilings and large skylights give the space a remarkable feeling of airiness, and its wooden floors and built-in cabinets provide a palette that is at once warm, welcoming, and modern. Angled walls and cabinets separate space casually, setting an informal and relaxed mood. Upstairs, a spacious open terrace links the level's bedrooms.

TOP AND ABOVE Bedrooms open directly out onto the broad second-floor terrace. | OPPOSITE A deep overhang enlarges the second floor's expansive terrace and shades the first floor.

STEFFEN LEISNER/SYNTAX 1+3=1 HOUSE
VENICE 2006

1 SPA | 2 POOL | 3 OFFICE | 4 DECK | 5 LIBRARY | 6 LIVING | 7 COURYARD | 8 RENTAL UNIT | 9 MEDITATION ROOM
10 MASTER SUITE | 11 ART STUDIO

SECOND FLOOR

FIRST FLOOR

ABOVE Exposed industrial materials mark the point where the new structure meets the frame of the original bungalow.

OPPOSITE Space set aside for a small courtyard helps the series of structures feel like a small village.

YOUNG L.A. ARCHITECTS Steffen Leisner, Ali Jeevanjee, and Phillip Trigas faced the considerable challenge of building a spacious, contemporary addition to a single-story, shingled bungalow in Venice that would fit gracefully into its urban neighborhood. The owners—a filmmaker and a multimedia artist—asked the architects to provide roughly 2,500 square feet of living, work, studio, and rental space on the long, narrow lot. By creating innovative, multistory additions on either side, the original structure could be kept intact.

These clearly differentiated new structures highlight the bungalow rather than dwarf it. Their sophisticated, smooth gray stucco exterior belies the inexpensive raw materials used in their construction. The final cost came in at just $199 per square foot. To the left of the bungalow, which sits sideways on the thin lot, the architects built a long concrete pool and added a new two-story structure that contains a small carved-out front porch, an office, and a second-floor meditation studio. The bungalow's east wall was removed to connect it directly to a new 1,000-square-foot structure containing a sunken living room with 12-foot ceilings and a second-floor bedroom. Farther east and separated by a courtyard, the firm built a new, freestanding, 1,065-square-foot structure that houses a small rental apartment and a tall second-floor artist's loft.

The flow of spaces is remarkably fluid; the entrance hall, kitchen, and living room occupy the same open plan. The striking new geometries succeed in adding drama, increase usable interior and exterior space, facilitate light penetration, and suit Venice's often quirky building codes—which, among other things, call for several parking spots on the site. All structures combine to create a miniature village of sorts that fits in well with the scale and roof lines of the surrounding neighborhood.

ABOVE High ceilings, industrial materials, and concrete floors give the rental unit the feel of an artist's studio. | OPPOSITE The meditation room is minimally appointed.

1 STUDIO | 2 GALLERY | 3 LIVING ROOM | 4 DINING ROOM | 5 BEDROOM | 6 DECK

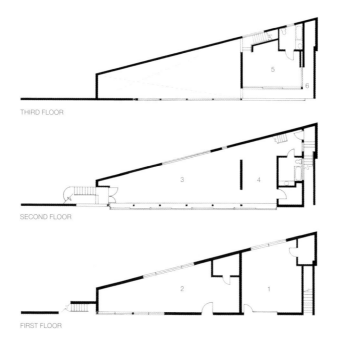

THIRD FLOOR

SECOND FLOOR

FIRST FLOOR

ABOVE Simple masonry blocks in various colors endow the space with personality.

OPPOSITE The double-height living space is filled with light thanks to a long band of horizontal windows on one side and a large, square window on the other.

LLOYD RUSSELL, MEMBER OF A RISING generation of architect/developers in San Diego, built this distinctive structure that locals call the "Triangle Building" after its shape, which is defined by an angled, narrow site in San Diego's Little Italy, adjacent to rumbling Interstate 5. Russell, in contrast, refers to it himself as the "R3 Building" because it was his third major built project.

The 1,600-square-foot, three-level structure appears almost impossibly thin when viewed from certain angles. Its eclectic facade is clad with unevenly molded concrete, multicolored concrete masonry units, and a staggered wood screen that references the plywood formwork used to cast the structure. On the first floor, Russell created a small gallery and office, fronted by a row of large windows.

The 20-foot-high living space above is also clad in exposed masonry blocks. This large room incorporates a kitchen, living, and dining space. West-facing windows cantilever out almost two feet, making it feel larger, while high clerestory windows bring in balanced light from above. A heavy drawbridge window made of 1-inch-thick glass opens the entire space. Behind the living area, a partial wall creates a dark, cozy media room. A narrow staircase leads up to an upper mezzanine bedroom, with sliding glass doors that in turn lead to a wraparound balcony providing splendid views of the bay and downtown San Diego. The airport is also extremely close by, so the architect used deep overhangs on the west elevation, mechanical ventilation, and double-glazed, heavy-duty windows to mitigate the sound from airplanes.

1 LIVING/DINING | 2 BEDROOM | 3 STUDY LOFT | 4 MASTER BEDROOM | 5 ROOF DECK

FIRST FLOOR

SECOND FLOOR

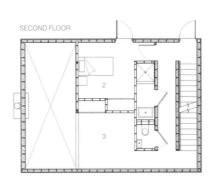

THIRD FLOOR

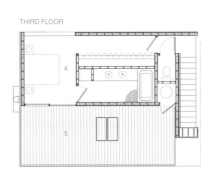

ABOVE A sliding door in the master bedroom provides quick access to a large deck and panoramic views of the neighborhood.

OPPOSITE Expansive windows bring the backyard's lush foliage into the living/dining space.

THIS RESIDENCE ON A TIGHT URBAN SITE measures only 1,500 square feet, but it feels much larger due to its strategic use of space, light, and natural surroundings. Architects Olivier Touraine and Deborah Richmond constructed the house for themselves several years after securing the 5,600-square-foot lot. The couple decided to build up, since local zoning rules prevented building out.

Their three-story house is clad with large expanses of clear glass, polycarbonate, and corrugated-metal panels that shift between horizontal, diagonal, and vertical configurations, creating a memorably varied composition. The architects made the most of the small outdoor spaces around the house, planting lush native vegetation and creating a small stone-clad patio, a gravel courtyard, and timber-floored balconies for the second and third floors. The lofty open-plan living room, which reaches to 18 feet at one point, features large, clear windows and sliding doors that further strengthen the house's connection to the outdoors. The house stays cool with the help of carefully planned cross-ventilation, shade from surrounding trees, and Mylar-lined curtains that reflect heat.

Pragmatic spaces are gathered in the center of each floor, including the kitchen—with integrated waferboard-clad appliances and cupboards—stairways, closets, bathrooms, and built-ins. Bedrooms and an office are organized along narrow hallways on the upper two floors. The architects, who only spent $250 per square foot on the project, eschew air conditioning and spend most of their time on the open first floor or one of the outdoor balconies. They feel that devoting most of the project to the enjoyment of the naturally pleasant California climate made more sense than maximizing indoor space.

MICHELE SAEE LINNIE HOUSE
VENICE 2005

1 LIVING ROOM | 2 DINING ROOM | 3 GARAGE | 4 MASTER BEDROOM | 5 STUDY | 6 BEDROOM | 7 STUDIO

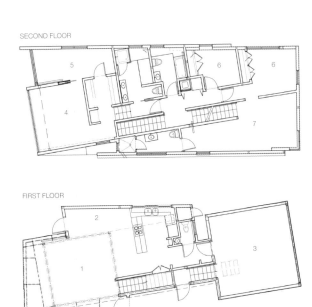

SECOND FLOOR

FIRST FLOOR

ABOVE The house's steel frame angles downward, focusing views on the canal.

OPPOSITE Furnishings with rounded, amoebalike forms contrast with the house's linear frame.

SITED ON VENICE'S PEACEFUL CANALS, this house built for two artists is all about layering. Wildly diverse elements successfully create a distinct whole. The two-story structure looks completely different from each side. From straight across the canal, the house looks to have a fairly ordinary rectangular form, but when approached from the adjacent canal path, the structure, which is sited diagonally on the lot to direct interior views toward a grove of trees across the waterway, starts to reveal a shifting geometry that projects in various unexpected directions.

The most prominent feature is a varnished, plywood-clad form that outlines the heart of the house: its first-floor living room and kitchen and second-floor master bedroom. The top half of the structure appears to be sliding toward the water; architect Michele Saee angled this segment's exterior walls down and around the level interior floor to place the bedroom's focal point on the canal. Concrete-clad spaces—including a study, rental suite, spare bedrooms, studio, garage, and storage spaces—project forcefully from this main volume. Since much of its first floor is clad in glass, the upper floors, clad in mostly opaque materials, attract the gaze first, creating an illusion that the house is floating over the water.

The house's open-plan, double-height living area is simply fitted with exposed wood beams and white plaster walls—a spare aesthetic maintained throughout. Unconventionally shaped rooms and strange nooks provide the visual interest. This unfolding form is perfectly suited to its artistic family that thinks very much outside the box.

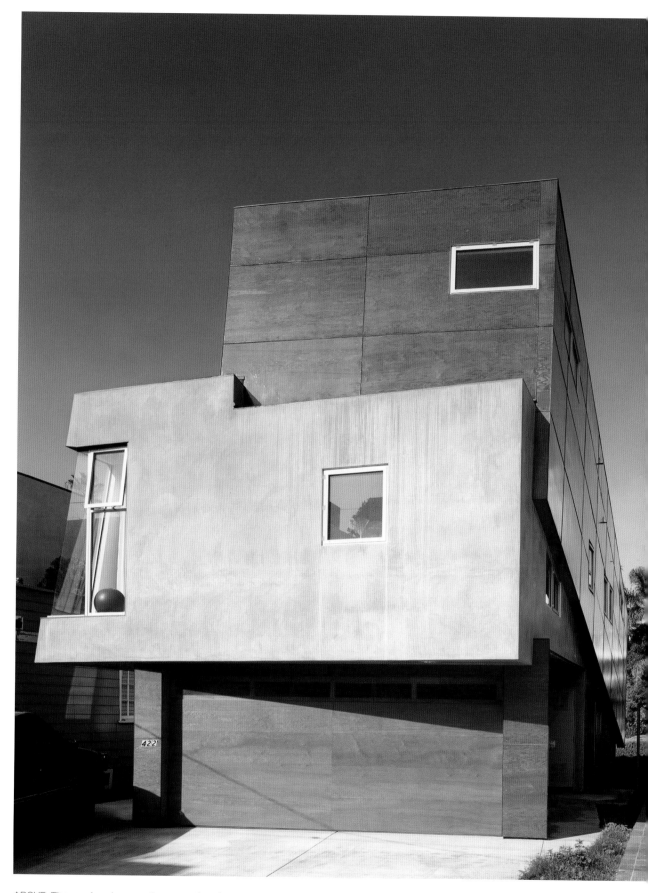

ABOVE The rear facade presents an arresting view of the structure's unconventional geometry. | OPPOSITE, ABOVE Bright colors enliven the industrial aesthetic and otherwise pure white space. | OPPOSITE, BELOW Thin wires form a unique support for the stair's railing.

RADICAL TRANSFORMATIONS

1 LIVING/DINING | 2 KITCHEN | 3 EATING ALCOVE | 4 LIBRARY/HALL | 5 OFFICE | 6 MEDIA ROOM | 7 STORAGE | 8 GUEST BEDROOM
9 OUTDOOR DINING | 10 OUTDOOR LIVING ROOM | 11 POOL | 12 MASTER BEDROOM | 13 BEDROOM | 14 CLOSET | 15 SOAKING TUB

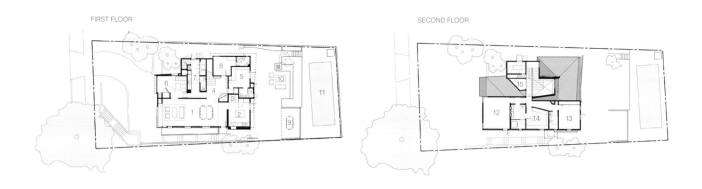

FIRST FLOOR

SECOND FLOOR

ABOVE Brightly colored window frames in various shapes and sizes inform the house's interior geometry and coordinate with decorative elements throughout.

OPPOSITE The colorful living room's expansive, projecting window focuses views on the neighborhood's many trees.

ARCHITECT WARREN TECHENTIN transformed a one-story stucco house in the Los Feliz neighborhood into a contemporary gem by merging old and new, creating seamlessly connected, textured spaces, and taking full advantage of the leafy setting. Sitting high above the street, the now two-story, 3,000-square-foot dwelling "feels like it is in the trees," Techentin says.

The facade, a combination of vertical and horizontal windows and redwood boards, forms a rain screen over the concrete-and-wood structure. Light and dark surfaces and flush and cantilevered cubes and planes create a vibrant, layered look and rhythm that defines the project. The architect merged his design with remnants of the original house, including a classic 1950s-era garage door and the shingle roof.

Inside, Techentin opened up the formerly cramped and jumbled house by removing walls and raising ceiling heights where possible. He also added a second floor and expanded the first. Rooms near the entry were merged into one spacious living/dining area. Here, a large horizontal window with a wide seat cantilevers slightly but feels as though it projects far into the yard.

The double height of the new wide hall brings abundant sunlight deep into the core of the house, making it a natural place to also position library shelving. Kitchen walls of white Polygal are translucent, allowing light to penetrate and turning the structural steel beams they surround into a wallpaper-like pattern of light and shadow. Upstairs, the harmonious mix of bright colors and materials such as plywood and poplar continues in the study and bedrooms. In the backyard, Techentin enhanced privacy by constructing a modern steel, glass, and wood fence around the courtyard and raised pool.

ABOVE Translucent walls transform the kitchen's steel beams into an enigmatic pattern of light and shadow. | OPPOSITE The dining room is full of contributions from artistic friends, including the colorful side table, main dining table and chairs, a botanical-print chandelier, and convex mirrors.

ABOVE Wallpaper in the eating alcove continues the kitchen's theme of black-on-white pattern.
OPPOSITE The double-height main hall adjacent to the stairway uses a lively shade of blue to unite
bookshelves and a whimsical chandelier.

DALY GENIK 823 PALMS
VENICE 2009

1 PATIO | 2 STUDY | 3 KITCHEN | 4 LIVING/DINING | 5 MASTER BEDROOM | 6 BEDROOM | 7 STUDIO

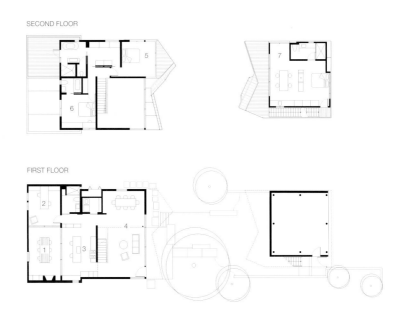

SECOND FLOOR

FIRST FLOOR

ABOVE The double height of the indoor patio allows ample sunlight to flood the space.

OPPOSITE Perforations in the main screen are revealed when backlit in the early evening.

THIS HOUSE HOLDS ITS OWN on an architecturally distinguished street that features projects by other well-known L.A. firms such as Steven Ehrlich and Marmol Radziner. The residence was once fairly banal: a mustard yellow stucco cube across a courtyard from a nondescript garage/rental unit. Daly Genik stripped both structures down to their studs, applied new hard plaster shells, shifted the main living quarters to the back of the lot, and created a new guest house in front.

The most remarkable introduction is the series of light gray perforated metal screens that hover in front of the structures. Set on angled aluminum frames, they reduce solar gain while allowing for ventilation—vital for a home without central air conditioning—while simultaneously providing privacy on the relatively tight urban lot. These protective canopies break open in strategic places to provide unimpeded views of the courtyard from timber-floored, second-story balconies.

The formerly cramped primary living area at the rear of the lot was opened by partially removing the upper floor to create one double-height space fronted by a window wall. A contemporary mixture of polished concrete, warm wood, and cork is used throughout the space. Behind the main living quarters, a courtyard gathering space recalls the indoor/out-door designs of Irving Gill, and James Turrell's skyspaces. Complete with its own kitchen, the self-sustaining guest house near the front of the property features a tall fireplace that serves as the open space's only divider. The architects reorganized the yard to make it more conducive to gatherings by filling it with new ipê benches and surrounding it with a lush combination of both native and nonnative plants.

ABOVE Breaks in the screen's surface on the second floor reveal views of the courtyard.
OPPOSITE A view of the screen's unique support structure.

STUDIO PALI FEKETE ARCHITECTS BEUTH RESIDENCE
WEST HOLLYWOOD 2005

1 GARAGE | 2 BILLIARDS | 3 MEDIA ROOM | 4 LIVING ROOM | 5 DINING ROOM | 6 LANDING | 7 DEN | 8 MASTER BEDROOM
9 SITTING ROOM | 10 BEDROOM | 11 LIBRARY

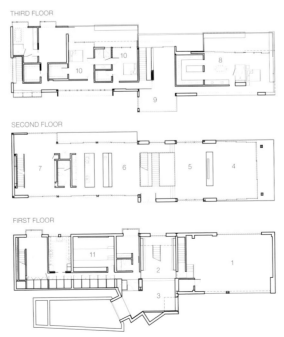

THIRD FLOOR

SECOND FLOOR

FIRST FLOOR

ABOVE The expansive kitchen and dining room was designed for entertaining a crowd.

OPPOSITE Floor-to-ceiling sliding glass doors and an uninterrupted plan give the living space a tremendous sense of openness.

SO FEW TRACES STILL EXIST of this site's original West Hollywood Hills house, with its stucco walls, angled roof, and uninspired archways, that it is difficult to believe the current structure is a renovation at all. What stands now is a long, thin, three-story residence that looks and feels like it is hovering in the air over the city.

Transparency defines the 9,200-square-foot residence, which abuts the crest of a steep hill to take full advantage of the site's expansive view. The main floor is clad so completely with floor-to-ceiling windows and sliding glass doors that it feels like one giant balcony. The circulation plan and floating staircases were carefully designed to create a continuous flow of space, and to avoid obstructing sightlines through the house to the outdoors.

The top floor contains personal spaces: the bedrooms with long, wide window boxes that frame the views, and a cantilevered sitting room that affords private, 180-degree views of everything from downtown's skyscrapers to the Getty Center. The ground level, carved out of the site's nearly 45-degree grade, is dedicated to leisure and entertainment, and contains the library, a gallery, and a screening room.

From the outside, the steel-framed house plays visual tricks. Because it rests on top of the glazed level below, the teak-clad top story appears to float. Its narrowness and length, broken up with window boxes and varied materials, not only allows for healthy cross breezes and views in all directions, but reinforces the impression that the house is projecting into the canyon below.

ABOVE Open stairs and catwalks contribute to the home's airy feeling. | OPPOSITE Solid surfaces appear to float above the glass-clad facade below.

TIGHE ARCHITECTURE TIGERTAIL
BRENTWOOD 2007

1 ENTRANCE | 2 GARAGE | 3 DEN | 4 LIVING ROOM | 5 MEDIA ROOM | 6 BEDROOM | 7 POOL | 8 DECK

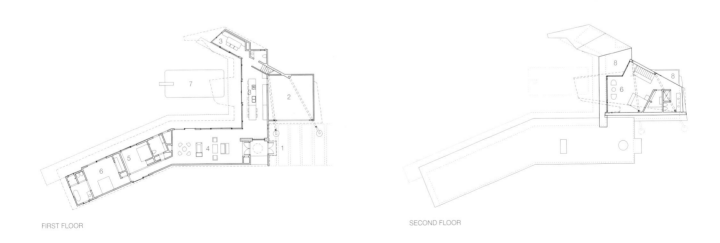

FIRST FLOOR

SECOND FLOOR

ABOVE The entryway is clad with light-colored, painted cement fiber-board panels, which contrast with the dark bonded metal above it.

OPPOSITE The streetside facade lies lower to fit in with the scale of the neighborhood.

THIS 3,200-SQUARE-FOOT RESIDENCE is an extreme makeover of a 1940s ranch house, which has been transformed from a cluttered, nondescript building into an open, light-filled, inspiring place to live. Architect Patrick Tighe maintained the original house's low-lying structure, which wraps around a green yard and small pool. The site provides a wonderful view of rolling Bundy Canyon and the Getty Center perched high in the distance.

The new iteration is wrapped in a layered and bonded steel skin typical of Tighe's ultramodern aesthetic. He opened up and merged rooms, and fitted walls with floor-to-ceiling sliding glass windows. Bamboo floors create an inviting warmth that offsets the modern lines around them. A photovoltaic trellis over the living spaces provides electricity for the house while also delineating and shading an outdoor room on the rooftop.

The house's focal point is the second-floor master suite and study, built above the entrance, garage, and kitchen. The tall, angled structure is supported by three bent steel moment frames that straddle the original building. Also clad in bonded steel, the folding space resembles a soaring wing from the front or side, its roof projecting beyond the edge of the house and pointing toward the view beyond. The interior of this upper-level space—including its ceiling—is lined with wood, blurring the distinction between wall, ceiling, and floor. Whatever surfaces are not covered in wood are covered in glass, providing views on three sides of the canyon, the city, and sometimes the ocean—on a clear day. "You can spend all day in here and still feel like you've been outside," the owner says.

ABOVE The bedroom's walls and ceiling fold up like a wing, providing shade and shaping views of the canyon and mountains.
OPPOSITE Birch plywood clads the interior walls of the bedroom and bathroom, providing warmth in this very modern composition.

STEVEN LOMBARDI 330 NEPTUNE
ENCINITAS 2008

1 STORAGE | 2 LAUNDRY | 3 GARAGE | 4 MEDIA ROOM | 5 OFFICE/BEDROOM | 6 GARDEN/PATIO | 7 ROCK GARDEN
8 MASTER BEDROOM | 9 BEDROOM | 10 LIVING/DINING | 11 DECK

MAIN FLOOR

GROUND FLOOR

ABOVE Woods warm up the
living space.

OPPOSITE The third-floor
addition to the house's front
end provides views of the ocean
and city.

IT WAS THIS SITE, rather than the structure on it, which first caught architect Steven Lombardi's attention. The house was a very ordinary 1950s dwelling, but it commanded a breathtaking view over a bluff along Encinitas's popular Stone Steps Beach. His extensive renovation focused on reorienting interior spaces to fully engage the wonderful setting.

The house's exterior was brought up to date with an alternating stucco and grooved aluminum facade, mahogany window frames, and a sleek standing seam metal roof. Lombardi also added a tall, 250-square-foot second story to the front end of the house, which allows light to pour into the master bedroom and creates a beaconlike lookout with 360-degree views of the neighborhood and the beach. The addition's projecting, pitched rafters echo the gabled design of the original house; this pattern is also used to top the new front entrance and opens sightlines from the front door through to the ocean.

Inside, traces of the original house are scant. New bamboo floors and maple and fir walls add warmth to the main living areas. The original 8-foot-high drop ceilings were opened and brought to almost twice that height. To hold up the new Douglas fir ceilings, the architect created a system of tie rods, steel beams, and struts. Large floor-to-ceiling sliding glass doors open the living room directly onto the adjacent beach, and a recycled wood deck projects over the bluff. The master bedroom is fitted with a glass garage door that opens onto a peaceful garden floored with pebble aggregate concrete and surrounded by understated plantings.

ABOVE The addition's grooved profile emphasizes its verticality. | OPPOSITE Exposed rafters reinforce the facade's linear rhythm.

NEIL M. DENARI ARCHITECTS ALAN-VOO HOUSE

CULVER CITY 2007

1 GARAGE | 2 BEDROOM | 3 DINING ROOM | 4 MASTER BEDROOM | 5 PATIO | 6 LIVING ROOM

FIRST FLOOR

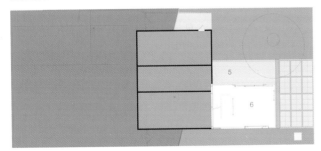

SECOND FLOOR

ABOVE The addition allowed an original wall to be removed, opening up the formerly cramped kitchen and connecting it with the dining room.

OPPOSITE Innovative shapes, detailing, and V-prop supports combine to define the addition's modern aesthetic.

THE FAMILY OF FIVE that owns this house was quickly running out of space in their aging 1,100-square-foot bungalow on Los Angeles's west side. So they asked Neil Denari—whose futuristic design for the nearby store l.a. Eyeworks they had admired—for an addition that would not only double their house's size, but also make it dramatically more contemporary.

Enlarged significantly by an excavation of the house's backyard, the architect's two-story, 1,000-square-foot expansion contains a simply furnished new living room on the first floor and a master bedroom and master bath on its second. The exposed, steel-framed structure seamlessly links to the original house via a tall, skylighted connector that permits clear views between the two buildings, helps balance light, and leaves room for a cantilevered stairway linking the addition's two floors. The borrowed space makes both buildings feel much larger. But the new sixteen-foot-wide addition is radically different, featuring bright, multitoned colors and unconventional lines. Extra-large windows invite the outdoors in, but since the space is surrounded by trees, it still feels private. Sliding glass doors on the ground floor open onto a new rock garden in the backyard.

The addition freed up significant space in the family's existing house, giving each child a separate bedroom and opening up the once-cramped living room and kitchen into a giant uninterrupted dining space. Curving lines were added to the walls in this space to link it visually to the addition. Long, ultrathin skylights reminiscent of fiber-optic cables—Denari calls them "sun tunnels"—provide extra natural light. The modern, unified spaces form an ideal refuge for this family that spends large amounts of time together.

ABOVE A new stair links the addition to the original structure's kitchen.
OPPOSITE The addition's double-height, skylit connector.

OPEN AND AIRY

ABRAMSON TEIGER ARCHITECTS KELLY HOUSE

BRENTWOOD 2006

1 ENTRY | 2 LIVING/DINING | 3 FAMILY ROOM | 4 BEDROOM | 5 PATIO | 6 MASTER BEDROOM | 7 OFFICE

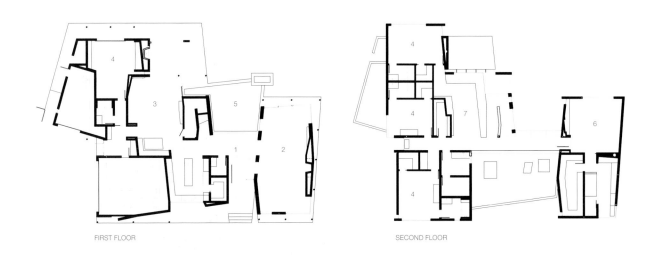

FIRST FLOOR

SECOND FLOOR

ABOVE A small pool, visible through a wall-sized window, is adjacent to the entrance hall.

OPPOSITE White second-floor walls project from the main facade; their color contrasts with the espresso and glass surfaces to establish a visual rhythm.

THIS HOUSE NEAR THE GETTY appears, at first, to be a typical modernist living space composed of a staggered series of three white cubes dotting the verdant landscape on which it sits. A closer look, however, reveals the subtle ways architectural firm Abramson Teiger interpreted that tradition to create a unique structure.

While totaling 5,000 square feet, this house does not feel bulky at all. One surface of each cubic volume is clad with espresso-colored, resin-coated wooden Trespa panels, warming the project, drawing attention to its unique geometry, and breaking down its scale. Solid second-floor walls contrast with the principally glass-clad first-floor and project outward from the main facade at several points. Thin pilotis support them, making the upper-level spaces appear weightless despite their large volumes.

The house has a welcoming, airy ambience inside. Spaces flow into one another seamlessly. The interior is warmed with natural wood finishes—ipê downstairs and bamboo upstairs—and with plentiful daylight. Ceilings are lofty and range from 9 to 11 feet in height, and outsized glass windows facing the backyard connect these tall spaces to the outdoors. Plentiful glass also contributes to the open feeling, as seen in the broad landing that separates the three cubes on the upper level. In some places, this house is transparent from front to back. The landscape design, by Steve Silva, begins with a small pond adjacent to the front of the house. The gently sloping site rises to meet a large pool behind the house that is framed by a lush, grassy yard.

ABOVE The sitting room looks out over the verdant backyard. | OPPOSITE Numerous staggered planes add interest to the facade.

ABOVE A cubic volume that projects from the main body of the house provides additional square footage and an alternate view of the yard and neighborhood. | OPPOSITE The double-height stairwell allows room for tall, glazed surfaces.

GRIFFIN ENRIGHT ARCHITECTS POINT DUME RESIDENCE

MALIBU 2007

1 ENTRY | 2 LIVING/DINING | 3 LIBRARY/OFFICE | 4 MEDIA ROOM | 5 GARAGE | 6 GUEST BEDROOM | 7 PORCH | 8 POOL
9 FIRE PIT | 10 PATIO | 11 TERRACE | 12 MASTER BEDROOM

FIRST FLOOR

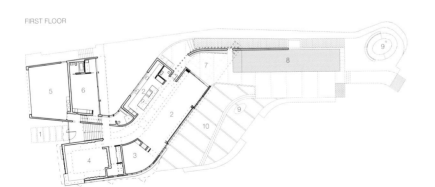

SECOND FLOOR

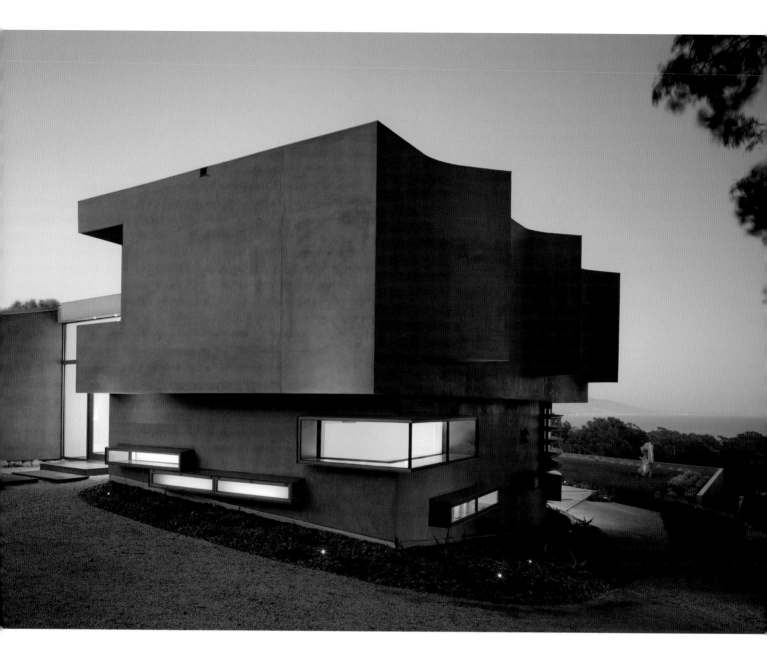

ABOVE Curved peel-aways on the facade direct views toward the ocean.

OPPOSITE A large brise-soleil that becomes the second-floor deck's railing provides shade, unifies the house's design, and creates a dynamic accent.

PERCHED ON TOP OF POINT DUME, a hilly promontory in Malibu, this house embraces the topographical features of its striking site. The building's S-shaped form echoes the curve of the Pacific coast below, and the plan gradually opens as it moves from the entrance through the living spaces. Irregularly and unexpectedly placed windows to the west and south direct views to specific vistas, and become larger as the plan unfurls. Both stories feature floor-to-ceiling sliding glass doors on their eastern facades that open wide to views of the ocean and distant mountains. On the first floor, these slide away to provide direct access to a generous patio, fire pit, and pool off the living/dining area. On the second floor, one full wall of the master bedroom can be similarly erased, leading to a broad deck that resembles the prow of a ship. Large brise-soleils and strategic siting minimize glare and solar gain.

A series of curving walls and long, arched skylights direct breezes and sun deep into the house's core. Rooms flow smoothly into each another, reinforcing the organic design. Shafts of light stretch across several rooms at a time, and view corridors establish sightlines through the entire house. The interior is warmed with rosewood and fired acacia fittings, walls, and floors. Polished concrete was used for both the living room and broad adjacent patio to reinforce the space's connection to the outdoors. In the yard, desert flora and a terraced hardscape echo the sinuous curves and warm colors of the house.

ABOVE The chandelier, by artist Chris Lehrecke, was modeled after bells found in a Thai monastery. | OPPOSITE A dramatic light box in the living room is made of resin panels inlaid with bear grass.

ABOVE Intersecting curves in the master bedroom echo the lines found throughout the house. | OPPOSITE Skylights carved into the second-floor entryway light the curved hall. | OVERLEAF One full wall of the master bedroom slides away, providing direct access to the wide deck.

1 ENTRY | 2 DINING/LIBRARY | 3 LIVING | 4 DJ BOOTH | 5 PATIO | 6 DECK | 7 MASTER BEDROOM | 8 GUEST ROOM/OFFICE

FIRST FLOOR

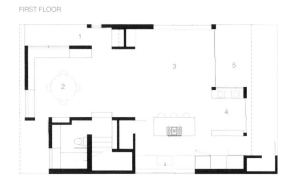

SECOND FLOOR

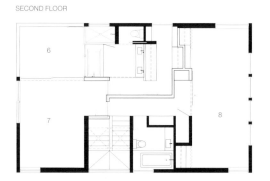

ABOVE A courtyard outside the master bedroom adds valuable outdoor living space.

OPPOSITE Brightly colored furniture and walls pop against the otherwise neutral interior.

THIS EXCEPTIONALLY LIVABLE, BRIGHT HOUSE was designed for the creative director of a large advertising firm. The house exudes personality both in its dramatic use of color and in its inventive manipulation of traditional design tropes. Established rules of residential architecture are subtly broken—scales, styles, and materials are mixed, and the limits of permeability are tested.

The lower portion of the facade is clad with dark cement board panels and the upper with an envelope of white vinyl-coated, standing seam metal. Such a contrasting combination—along with the upper floor's overhanging, slightly pitched roof and textured metallic surface reminiscent of shiplapped planks—creates the sensation that the second floor is floating. The metallic surface is actually fabricated from the same steel used on many ship hulls, and it was also chosen here for its salt- and moisture-resistant properties.

Inside, the house exemplifies architect Barbara Bestor's "Bohemian Modern" aesthetic. Raw plywood, built-in cabinetry, furniture and artwork created by Bestor's friends, and vividly colored walls combine to create a high-design but down-to-earth residence. Each facade on the structure's first floor features large windows or pivoting doors that open wide to the outdoors, while strategically placed landscaping in the front and an enclosed "outdoor living room" in the back maintain privacy.

In order to allow light to permeate deep into the interior on the second floor, bedroom walls were capped at 8 feet, and glass was installed between the top of each and the ceiling to completely close off individual spaces. A large balcony carved into the master bedroom provides private, splendid views of the neighborhood, and adds even more usable outdoor space.

ABOVE A double-height window in the brightly colored stairwell provides a visual connection to the neighborhood. | OPPOSITE Glass dividers placed between the tops of walls and the ceiling allow light to penetrate deep into the second floor while buffering noise between rooms.

STEVEN EHRLICH 700 PALMS RESIDENCE
VENICE 2005

1 COURTYARD | 2 POOL | 3 LIVING/DINING | 4 GARAGE | 5 BEDROOM | 6 STUDIO/LIVING SPACE | 7 DECK
8 MASTER BEDROOM | 9 LIBRARY

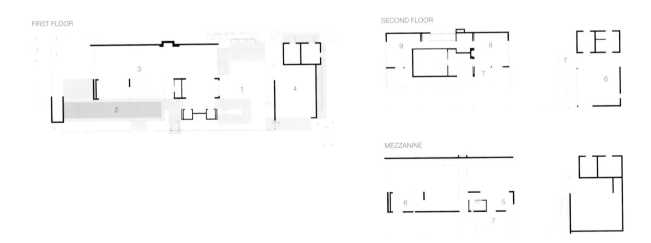

FIRST FLOOR

SECOND FLOOR

MEZZANINE

ABOVE This poolside opening, one of three carved into the facade of the house, allows light and breezes to penetrate.

OPPOSITE Weathered steel on the facade contrasts with the warm, welcoming finishes on the interior.

CLAD WITH AN IMPOSING COMBINATION of Cor-Ten steel sheets, copper siding, and stucco that conceals the lightness of the interior, this house on a narrow corner lot fits well within the historically gritty aesthetic of Venice, a neighborhood that has shifted in recent years from a depressed area to an upscale arts haven. The simple form of the solid exterior provides privacy—enhanced by panels of brightly colored scrim hung from a steel frame that can be raised and lowered in response to foot traffic or the sun's intensity—and defines the volume of the 16-foot-high, open-plan living area inside.

The surprisingly light-filled, warm living/dining space is lined with exposed concrete masonry blocks and dark steel sheets that serve as a visual counterpoint to the warm wood stairs and exposed ceiling rafters. The combination gives the room a modern, edgy personality well suited to the site. Each of the two long sides is fitted with industrial sliding doors that open the room wide to the yard. Mezzanine-level living spaces and a bedroom overlook the first-floor space. The master bedroom and a spacious steel balcony occupy the third level, and are linked to the main space via a glass catwalk. A two-floor structure containing a studio and guest suite was constructed across the yard from the main house.

Sustainable elements include polished concrete floors that absorb the sun's rays to reduce dependence on traditional heating methods in winter, operable windows and sliding doors that encourage natural ventilation, low-maintenance recycled construction materials, and careful solar shading.

ABOVE A uniquely crafted stair also provides shelving in the living space.
LEFT The landscape becomes a part of the house when an outsize door slides away.

ABOVE Brightly colored scrim panels shade the lap pool from direct rays. | OPPOSITE An open plan allows a view through the house, courtyard, and into the adjacent studio.

JONATHAN SEGAL LEMPERLE RESIDENCE
LA JOLLA 2008

1 ENTRY HALL | 2 WINDOW TO LOWER LEVEL | 3 LIVING/DINING | 4 MEDIA ROOM | 5 BEDROOM | 6 LIVING SPACE | 7 DECK
8 MASTER BEDROOM SUITE

SECOND FLOOR

THIRD FLOOR

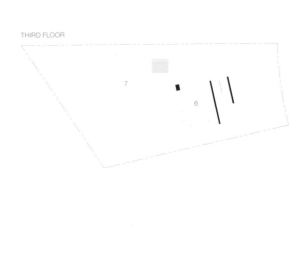

FIRST FLOOR

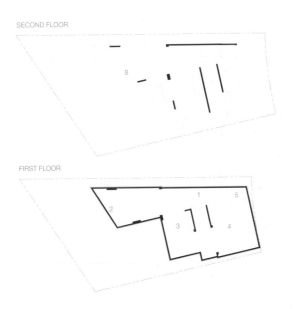

ABOVE A glass segment in the living room floor filters natural light into the basement below.

OPPOSITE Expansive views from the master bedroom toward the ocean.

THIS HOUSE, ONE OF JUST A FEW projects architect and developer Jonathan Segal has completed for a private client, takes advantage of a unique site just feet from La Jolla's Bird Rock Beach. The structure is comprised of a four-level, cast-in-place concrete tower whose oceanfront facades are almost completely clad in ¾-inch thick, UV-treated, floor-to-ceiling glass. A computerized system controls sunshades according to the time of day and the angle of the sun to keep the 4,800-square-foot interior comfortable. The facade facing away from the beach provides privacy and architectural drama as its thick, angular, Cor-Ten steel and concrete frame unfolds.

Angling to fit its trapezoidal lot and to accommodate required setbacks, the L-shaped house arranges public living spaces on the basement and first-floor levels, private on the second, and an office and open deck on the third. A partial roof over the deck, which is covered in solar panels, provides shading and rain cover without breaking the beach's strict 30-foot height limit. Segal also creatively augmented living space on the restricted lot by designing a 2,000-square-foot basement that includes a deep light well/patio complete with deck, fire trough, and water feature. Glass set into the first level's floor also brings natural light into the underground areas.

Green technology was incorporated into the home wherever possible: low voltage lighting is used throughout, the floors are radiantly heated, solar energy is gathered, and a subsurface drainage system collects and recycles ground water.

TOP AND ABOVE The basement-level dining room and bar receive natural light and ventilation from a deep light well/patio.
OPPOSITE One of the house's several fire troughs creates a border between land and sea.

ENVIRONMENTALLY MINDED

1 ENTRY | 2 LIVING/DINING | 3 BEDROOM | 4 STUDY | 5 MASTER BEDROOM | 6 BALCONY | 7 SMOKING BALCONY

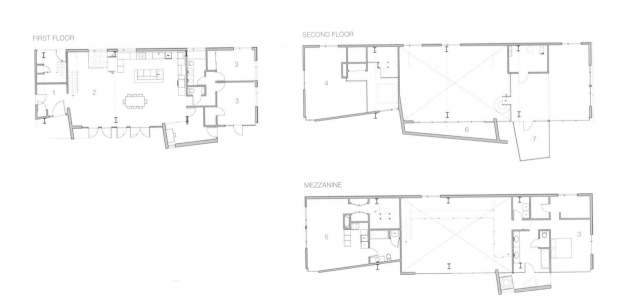

FIRST FLOOR

SECOND FLOOR

MEZZANINE

ABOVE A spiral stair to the top floor is one of many sculptural forms that lead the eye from one focal point to another.

OPPOSITE The facade is a study in contrasting materials—ordered shiplapped steel, irregular concrete surfaces, glass, and steel—that are alternately colorful, opaque, clear, and translucent.

THIS 3,800 SQUARE FOOT STRUCTURE, located on a quiet street in Culver City, is one of Whitney Sander's "Hybrid Houses," which combine prefabricated shell components with custom interior walls, systems, and finishes. It was erected in three weeks. According to the architect, the entire project cost only $130 per square foot, a miracle in Los Angeles. Its name comes from one of the owners' dogs, a Briard named Hobbes.

The facade is built on a frame of thick steel. Its infill includes a mosaiclike pattern of clear glass, colored acrylic panels, and unusually-angled sprayed concrete over Styrofoam beams. The complex composition was inspired from a cubist painting by Braque, the Aria of Bach. Environmentally responsible materials such as insulation made from shredded blue jeans and cabinets made of compressed sunflower seeds were not only integrated into the design, but purposefully left exposed. The structure also includes a passive heating and cooling system and a cistern for collecting and recycling rain water.

A short entry hall leads to an impressive 28-foot-tall living room surrounded by a suspended balcony. Its railing is inlaid with stalks of rice grass, furthering the environmental theme, and it is wide enough to be used for seating during regular chamber music concerts hosted by the owners, one of whom is a music critic. It receives dappled light from the transparent and translucent facade, and connects to a thin but verdant yard via a series of small glass doors. The room also contains a built-in kitchen with glazed concrete countertops and bright red off-the-shelf cabinets. A metallic spiral stair leads to a top floor study and wedge-shaped, cantilevered metal "smoking deck" that boasts uninterrupted views of the neighborhood and nearby hills.

ABOVE Alternating panes of translucent and clear glass in the bedroom create privacy but allow glimpses of the nearby hillsides. | OPPOSITE Circulation between the house's three stories follows a carefully designed procession of balconies and stairs.

OFFICE OF MOBILE DESIGN SEATRAIN
LOS ANGELES 2003

1 ENTRY | 2 LIVING ROOM | 3 UTILITY/LAUNDRY | 4 KOI POND | 5 LAP POOL | 6 LIBRARY | 7 MEDIA ROOM | 8 FOOT BRIDGE
9 GUEST HOUSE

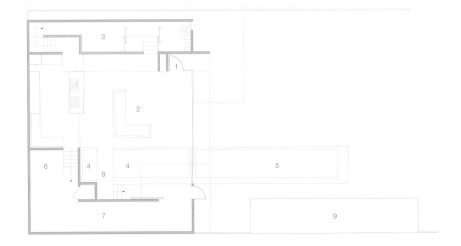

ABOVE The central living space is composed of an eclectic mix of materials—metals, woods, and stone—arranged in intersecting planes.

OPPOSITE A large window wall affords uninterrupted views of the garden.

THE IDEA OF BUILDING A HOUSE out of shipping containers is becoming familiar, though few architects manage it this elegantly and comfortably, especially for such an unexpected location. The residence is on a formerly empty industrial lot in L.A.'s Lincoln Heights section, on the edge of downtown and adjacent to the large arts cooperative called the Brewery. One of the Brewery's owners, Richard Carlson, commissioned the project and enlisted Brewery artists to build it. The team dug up existing concrete slabs and replaced them with a thick, wild combination of plants, which grow especially well since the site is on the original alluvial plain of the now asphalt-covered L.A. River. Jennifer Siegal, the project's architect and a former Brewery resident, calls the site the "enchanted garden" for its dense plantings and seclusion from the street.

The house is composed of four corrugated steel shipping containers, which had, like their uneven site, been sitting abandoned in the area—Siegal likes to say they were hibernating. The containers sit on top of each other in twos, separated by a living space roofed with a steel surface that tilts with the change in grade between the house's two sides. They are fronted by a facade of thick glass sheets that are abutted to create the illusion of a continuous glass wall. This eclectic middle space is the heart of the project.

The room's floor alternates between concrete and dark cherry wood, and it is enlivened by a succession of changes in levels and an indoor koi pond fed by a waterfall made of stacked flagstone. The four multipurpose containers hold equally adaptable bedroom/bathroom, entertainment room/library, dining room/study, and laundry/mechanical spaces.

ABOVE The breakfast nook in the kitchen is adjacent to a footbridge that leads to the upper level. | OPPOSITE An interior koi pond injects a serene note into the lively architectural composition.

ABOVE An upper-level bedroom peeks into the main living space through a thin central window.
OPPOSITE A view from the footbridge reveals the main living space's large volume.

1 LIVING ROOM | 2 DINING ROOM | 3 BEDROOM | 4 STUDY | 5 LAUNDRY | 6 WATER POND | 7 BAMBOO PLANTER
8 MASTER BEDROOM | 9 PATIO | 10 ROOF | 11 SKYLIGHT

FIRST FLOOR

SECOND FLOOR

RATHER THAN CONSIDERING SUSTAINABLE components and outdoor living spaces after planning a main structure, as is often the case, architect Lawrence Scarpa instead used them to actually direct the form of this fascinating dwelling. The project is technically an addition to a 1920s bungalow in Venice. The architect removed the bungalow's south wall, eliminating its living room to replace it with enlarged kitchen and dining areas, and converted one bedroom into a study. To its south, he added an airy two-story structure of tilt-up concrete containing a sunken living room, a second-floor master suite, and a combined bath/utility room.

The project's "solar umbrella" wraps the addition's roof and west elevation. Consisting of a translucent canopy of eighty-nine grid-connected, razor-thin solar panels, the four-kilowatt system generates nearly all the electricity the occupants use, and serves as a sunshade for the top floor deck and the house's defining visual detail. Other green elements include a storm water retention basin, radiant heating, a composting system, fly ash concrete, and recycled materials.

The rest of the 1,900-square-foot project is a textbook example of Southern California indoor/outdoor architecture. Its rectilinear frame—crisscrossed vertically and horizontally with light-colored concrete and darker steel beams—has unusually high ceilings and outsized industrial sliding doors, so every room is blanketed with light and air. On the addition's upper story, an open porch permits views straight through from both sides of the street. The porch leads to the tucked-away master suite, which is shielded from the sun's intense rays by steel and recycled broom fiber screens. Spaces flow together and into the original house: children like to jump from the bungalow's kitchen down onto the addition's couch, over the coffee table, and straight out into house's yard.

ABOVE A sightline straight through the kitchen to the backyard contributes to the house's open, loftlike feeling.
OPPOSITE The central stair's perforated steel construction renders it close to invisible from underneath.

TAALMAN KOCH ARCHITECTURE OFF-GRID ITHOUSE

PIONEERTOWN 2007

1 MECHANICAL | 2 STORAGE | 3 MASTER BEDROOM | 4 BEDROOM | 5 COURTYARD | 6 STORAGE/LAUNDRY | 7 LIVING/DINING

ABOVE Floor-to-ceiling windows provide uninterrupted views of the unique landscape.

OPPOSITE The continuous glass facade is shaded with a gridded decal system.

BUILT AS A WEEKEND RETREAT by Los Angeles architects Linda Taalman and Alan Koch, this modular house sits on a rocky five-acre site just outside Joshua Tree National Park, two hours east of L.A. Miles from the nearest electric tower, the isolated location was the perfect place to experiment with off-the-grid technology and prefab construction.

The 1,200-square-foot house has a simple rectangular floor plate interrupted only by two small courtyards, which contain an entrance plaza and a small relaxation space. Formica-clad cabinetry helps partition the house's two main spaces: a living room/kitchen and a bedroom. A large overhang shades the building's floor-to-ceiling windows, as does a dark, patterned vinyl decal grid applied to the glazing. To complete the sense of utter seclusion, the bedroom was nestled between a small hill and a cluster of acacia trees.

The architects used a mix of prefabricated and on-site construction techniques. The aluminum framing, steel roof, cabinets, glazing, and doors were built off-site and shipped to the plot in pieces. The house's concrete foundation and electrical and plumbing systems were fabricated on-site. Eight rooftop solar panels provide hot water, radiant under floor heating, and all electricity.

With the design's simplicity and prefabricated elements, the architects anticipate that it will be a good candidate for mass production. While trying to regulate the first few iterations of the prototype, the couple has learned to let potential clients take advantage of the system's inherent malleability, letting them place modules and courtyards in several different configurations than those they had originally intended, to meet the needs of different topographies and sites.

ABOVE A hanging sculptural fireplace's curved form adds visual contrast to the rectilinear structure. | OPPOSITE Tilted solar panels above the courtyard provide shade as well as electricity.

MOUNTAINSIDE RETREATS

AGPS.ARCHITECTURE TOPANGA RANCH
TOPANGA CANYON 2004

1 KITCHEN | 2 DINING ROOM | 3 OFFICE | 4 LIVING ROOM | 5 DRESSING ROOM | 6 BEDROOM

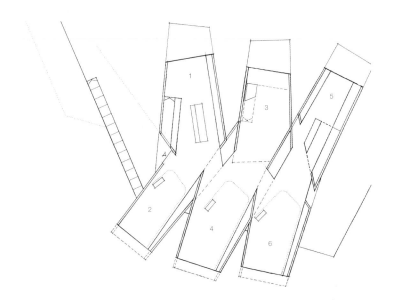

ABOVE Extensive landscaping
resulted in a new access
road, retaining walls, a paddock,
gardens, and orchards.

OPPOSITE The three "fingers"
of the house project over the
polycarbonate clad garage and
into the landscape.

SITUATED IN ONE OF SOUTHERN CALIFORNIA'S HILLIEST—and driest—coastal
canyons, this residence takes particularly conscientious advantage of its site. The
dwelling is divided into three interconnected "fingers" or "trinoculars," as architect Sarah
Graham calls them, which separate eating, living, and sleeping areas into distinct zones.
The three long elements are glazed on each end but primarily solid on the sides, to focus
attention on distinct views that are alternately panoramic and focused on a certain feature
of the topography.

By cladding the entire building with a rubber roofing product called Sarnafil, the firm
created a continuously smooth surface. Its color also echoes reddish tones found in the
landscape. A braced steel frame built atop a concrete base gives the house structure
and gives it a high fire rating, an important consideration for a site previously ravaged by
the famous 1993 Topanga fire. Other fire safety measures included clearing nearby brush
and selecting fire- and drought-resistant plants for the yard.

Inside, the light-filled tall white spaces with their unique wedged geometries weave in
and out of each other seamlessly, with only informal dividers. The eating wing contains
a kitchen on one end and a dining room on the other; the living segment contains a long
living room, office, and lofted guest space; and the third "finger" contains the master
bedroom suite. Built-in beechwood storage walls were constructed into the side of each
segment to reduce the need for freestanding furnishings that could clutter the interior's
clean, minimal lines. In many places, cabinetry and dividers have been given cutaway
corners, continuing the theme of sophisticated angles.

While the light-filled living room and guest room connect, they direct views in very different directions.

TOP The kitchen's angled cabinetry drives gazes to the outdoors. | ABOVE The master bath's unique geometry angles light from clerestory windows into the rest of the house. | OPPOSITE, ABOVE Light filters through translucent walls to penetrate the interior. | OPPOSITE, BELOW Concrete was selected as a primary building material for its resistance to fire.

LORCAN O'HERLIHY ARCHITECTS JAI HOUSE
CALABASAS 2004

1 LIVING/DINING | 2 KITCHEN | 3 FAMILY ROOM | 4 PANTRY | 5 POOL | 6 BEDROOM | 7 PATIO | 8 YOGA STUDIO
9 MASTER BEDROOM | 10 OFFICE | 11 KOI POND

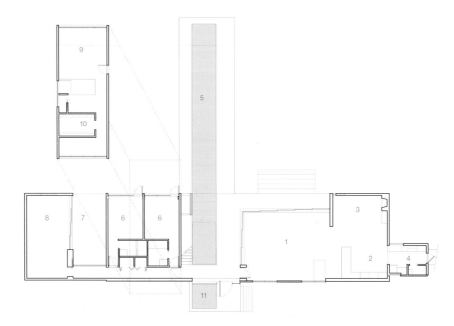

ABOVE The living room sits adjacent to the entry and the long pool that bisects the house.

OPPOSITE A second-floor volume perpendicular to the rest of the structure contains the master bedroom suite and cantilevers far over the first-floor spaces.

A PERFECT EXAMPLE OF ARCHITECTURAL INNOVATION arising from a simple concept, this striking residential project essentially consists of two long, rectilinear concrete volumes that intersect at a perpendicular angle. The straightforward arrangement of spaces belies the sophistication of their relation to each other and their intimate relatnionship to the outdoors—it is less a house in the traditional sense than a colony of individual spaces with discrete functions. The owners, a nature-loving couple, originally envisioned a house on a steep site, which they equated with dramatic views. Architect Lorcan O'Herlihy convinced them to build on this flat lot instead, to provide more usable yard space. It overlooks the dramatic Santa Monica Mountains, giving the family the vistas they hoped for while enabling him to incorporate permeable features that erase the distinction between indoors and outdoors.

Several unexpected elements distinguish this structure. The front door, for example, opens not into an enclosed entryway, but onto an outdoor patio and a 70-foot-long narrow swimming pool that bisects the plan. Public living areas are located to the right, private spaces to the left. The combined living room/kitchen space has sliding glass walls and doors that allow it to open up completely to the backyard, while clerestory windows and frosted glass panels maintain privacy on the facade facing the street. The hallway leading to the bedrooms also receives light from a similarly slender band of windows, though unconventionally placed at ground level. A small gravel courtyard separates the bedrooms along this hall from the last room in the wing, which is used as a yoga studio. All private rooms, like the public spaces, have direct access to the outdoors.

A riserless exterior stair next to the pool leads to the second-floor master bedroom suite. Its black plaster surface juxtaposes dramatically with the white used elsewhere, giving the volume definition. An adjacent but freestanding large white wall was constructed as an outdoor movie screen—the family watches films while seated on the roof.

Corner glass doors open the living room to the yard.

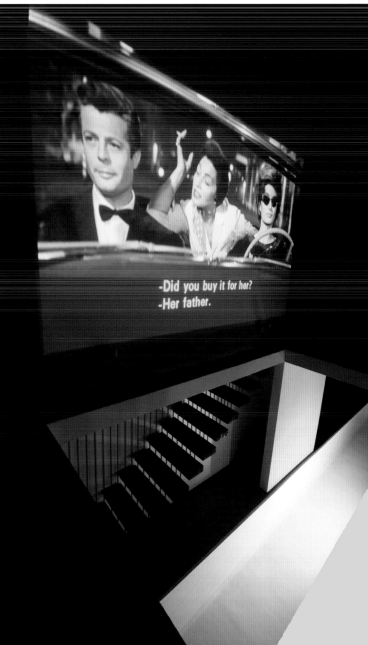

TOP Light infuses the main kitchen/dining area. | ABOVE The master bedroom integrates bath spaces directly into the sleeping area. | OPPOSITE An opening in the roof mimics the shape of the pool beneath it; residents can view outdoor films projected onto a solid white wall.

OLSON SUNDBERG KUNDIG ALLEN ARCHITECTS
MONTECITO RESIDENCE
MONTECITO 2008

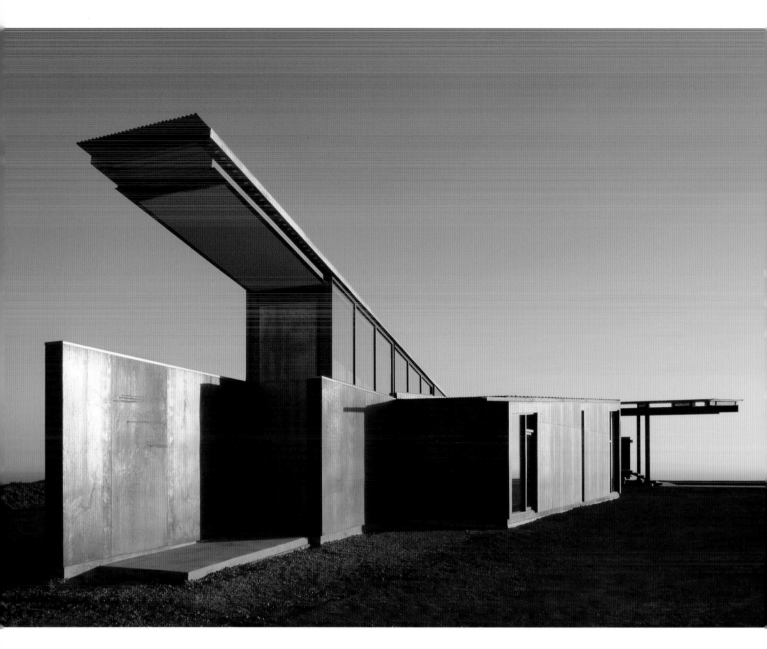

1 ENTRY | 2 GUEST BEDROOM | 3 OFFICE/GUEST BEDROOM | 4 LIVING/DINING | 5 MASTER BEDROOM

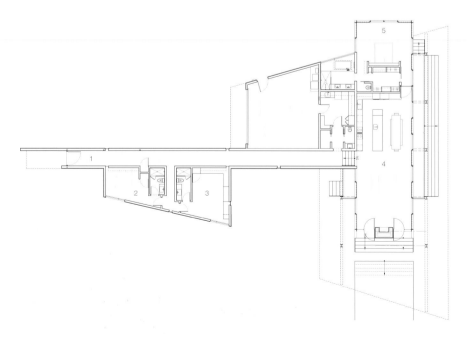

ABOVE Flora in the backyard is kept closely cropped in case of wildfire.

OPPOSITE The angled "tail" draws naturally cool sea breezes through the house.

A THICK LAYER OF STEEL CLADDING covers this mountainside residence, but despite this imposing material, the house merges gracefully into its rugged environment. Cor-Ten steel was chosen for its ability to oxidize into a rough, rust-colored surface that would blend into the reddish earth tones of its surroundings. The color will deepen, integrating the house even further into the landscape as it continues to oxidize. Architect Tom Kundig chose steel for more than aesthetic reasons—it is fire-resistant as well. To protect the structure as much as possible from any wildfires, the land was also cleared of brush and planted with hardy, fire-resistant vegetation.

The T-shaped house is divided into two main elements. One is the narrow "spine," a hall lined with clerestory windows that leads from the entrance to the guest bedroom, office, and finally into the main body of the house. The other is a wide living area overlooking the ocean, a loftlike space full of floor-to-ceiling glass that contains the living room, kitchen, and master bedroom. Both elements' functions can be determined from the exterior: the spine's structure finishes with an upswept "tail" that shades the entry and draws hot air away from the house. The living area's roof is also marked by a similar but wider rise, or "wing," which shades the entire floor-to-ceiling glass facade, keeping the interior cool.

Simply furnished interiors rely on the magnificent landscape for decoration. The house was also kept to 3,500 square feet to quietly complement, rather than overwhelm, this remarkable site high above the sea.

The main living/dining space was placed at the western edge of the house to take advantage of sunset views over the ocean.

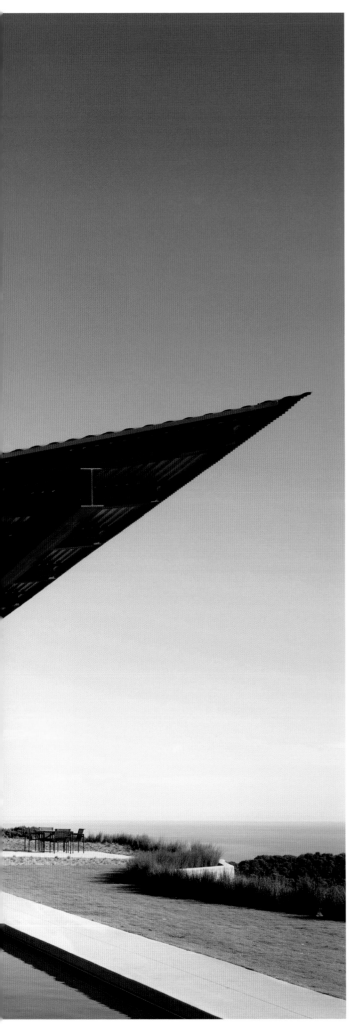

ABOVE The master bedroom cantilevers over the ground to promote air circulation on all sides. | LEFT The steel cladding will be allowed to oxidize to help the house blend into the landscape. | OVERLEAF The tall main door splits to adjust airflow through the house's long main hallway.

KANNER ARCHITECTS MALIBU 5

MALIBU 2006

1 PATIO | 2 FOYER | 3 LIVING ROOM | 4 DINING ROOM | 5 DECK | 6 MEDIA ROOM | 7 STUDY | 8 MASTER BEDROOM
9 WALK-IN CLOSET | 10 BEDROOM

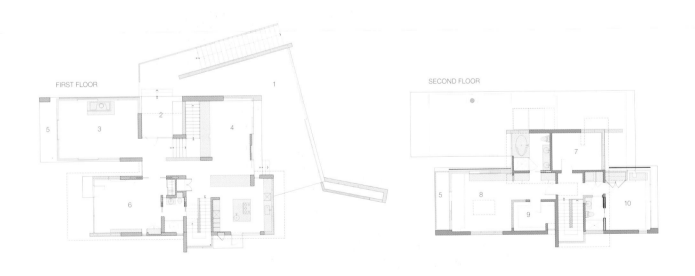

FIRST FLOOR

SECOND FLOOR

ABOVE Large roof planes hover over the glass walls, shading the interior spaces.

OPPOSITE C-shaped volumes interlock like a puzzle to create the house's distinctive exterior form.

SET INTO A CRAGGY HILLSIDE, this open, sculptural structure is full of interlocking planes, hovering ceilings, grooved wall details, offset forms, and broad openings that together form a single, permeable, puzzlelike house. The building melds high design with sustainable elements insisted upon by the owners—avid environmentalists—including passive ventilation, radiant heating, solar electric and thermal panels, and native vegetation in the yard.

Kanner Architects designed lofty cantilevers that jut far over first-story walls, increasing second-story living space and shading the interior without increasing the house's footprint on the land. A narrow patch of yard bisects the plan, allowing breezes to penetrate deep into the interior. Exterior components reference the intersecting planes of modernists such as Rudolph Schindler and Richard Neutra. The cladding, a deeply textured, troweled red stucco that helps distinctive "C" shapes of the facade to pop against the glazing, was brought back from Africa by architect Steven Kanner, and blends well with the earth tones of the California landscape.

Inside, the open first floor is organized around a lofty entrance core from which the kitchen, living and dining rooms, and media rooms radiate. Tall windows shaded by deep overhangs bring the outside in, making the surroundings a dominant feature of the house, particularly during windstorms and rainstorms. The second floor is comprised of a study and a master bedroom suite that perch lightly on the lower level. This openness, exposure, and focus on a site that is almost spiritual in its beauty has prompted the owners to give the house a second name, Canto Libre, meaning "song of freedom."

LEFT A side patio with views of the ocean leads to the main entrance on the house's northern side.
OPPOSITE From the dining room, the entire first floor can be seen.

ABOVE A contemporary fireplace is the only break in the livng room's wraparound views. | OPPOSITE The master bedroom's neutral palette highlights structural details.

1 BEDROOM | 2 KITCHEN/ENTRY | 3 LIBRARY

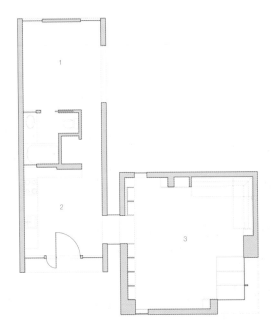

ABOVE A clean aesthetic in the kitchen contrasts with the thick, wild landscape just outside.

OPPOSITE A corner window provides a visual break in the otherwise vertical pattern of the facade.

TECHNICALLY A FREESTANDING ADDITION to a ranch house on a winding hilltop street in Beverly Hills, this project feels like a tropical retreat. Surrounded by a small reflecting pool and a staggered steppingstone walkway, the 850-square-foot structure appears to be floating on water as it is approached. Its two tall, adjoining, cube-shaped buildings peek out from an enveloping grove of surrounding trees but also blend into the natural environment thanks to their abstract, bladelike cladding of alternating light- and dark-green cement board panels that evoke the site's lush vegetation.

The addition's interior is designed to filter distractions from the world outside, while allowing focused, framed glimpses of it through carefully placed glazed surfaces. Many windows are at clerestory level, admitting sunlight and providing fleeting views of the swaying trees above, while others emulate the strong, narrow, vertical lines found on the exterior. The calming babble of the reflecting pond, whose runoff stream winds around the front of the structure, can be heard from each room.

The flow of Lago Vista's spaces is as fluid as the water surrounding it. Informal barriers, rather than full walls or doors, separate spaces. Originally planned as a single "contemplation room," the plan for the small cube grew to include a bedroom and bath for guests, and eventually a full kitchen for entertaining as well. The double-height library, defined by bright colors and an impressive wall of books, joins this space via a narrow bridge that crosses over a heavily planted green space. A cantilevered corner window with a glass floor directs views to the canyon in the distance, and creates the surreal feeling for occupants that they are floating above the slope that drops away steeply under their feet.

TOP Built-in cabinetry informally divides space. | ABOVE Dappled light from tall windows gently illuminates the bedroom. | OPPOSITE The library's ladder, windows, bookshelves, and closets all emphasize the structure's verticality.

ABOVE Wall-to-wall bookshelves in the library are interrupted only by a door to the kitchen. | OPPOSITE The entry hall leads to the yard and views over the valley.

PHOTOGRAPHY CREDITS

JIM BARTSCH 212–13, 215

RICHARD BARNES 130, 131, 132, 133, 134, 135

TIM BIES/OSKA 2–3, 214

PAUL BODY 160, 161, 162, 163, 164, 165

BENNY CHAN 14–15, 16, 17, 18 TOP, 18 BOTTOM, 19, 20–21, 58–59, 60, 61, 62, 63 TOP, 63 BOTTOM, 77, 94–95, 96, 97, 98, 99, 120–21, 123, 125, 136–37, 138, 139, 140–41, 142, 143, 144, 145, 222–23, 224, 225, 226, 227, 228, 229

JONN COOLIDGE 206, 207, 208–9, 211 TOP

GREY CRAWFORD 156, 157, 159

CHRISTOPHER CULLITON 64–65, 66, 67, 68, 69

JOHN ELLIS 146, 147, 148, 149, 150, 151

ART GRAY 4–5, 52, 53, 54, 55, 56–57, 108–9, 110, 111, 112 TOP, 112 BOTTOM, 113, 190, 191, 192, 193

DAVID HARRISON 70–71, 72, 73

DANIEL HENNESSY 174, 175, 178, 181

TODD HIDO 45

RAIMUND KOCH 80, 81, 82 TOP, 82 BOTTOM, 83

NIKOLAS KOENIG 216–17, 218, 219, 220, 221

JASPER JOHAL 210 RIGHT

DAVID LENA 128–29, 230, 232, 233, 236, 237

JOHN LINDEN 103, 104–5, 106, 107

STEVEN LOMBARDI 114–15, 116, 117, 118, 119

JUERGEN NOGAI 74, 75, 76

GENE OGAMI 42, 43, 44

ERHARD PFEIFFER 152, 153, 155, 158

ETHAN PINES 122, 124

JASON PREDOCK 34–35, 36, 37, 38, 39 TOP, 39 BOTTOM, 40–41

UNDINE PROHL 28, 29, 30, 31, 32 TOP, 32 BOTTOM, 33, 46, 47, 48, 49, 176, 177, 179, 180

MARVIN RAND 78, 79, 182, 183, 184, 185, 186, 187

SHARON RISEDORPH 168, 169, 170, 171, 172, 173

GREGG SEGAL 188–9

JULIUS SHULMAN AND JUERGEN NOGAI 100-101, 102, 154

ERIC STAUDENMAIER 22, 23, 24, 25, 26, 27 TOP, 27 BOTTOM, 86, 87, 88, 89, 90, 91, 92, 93, 196–97, 198, 199, 200–201, 202 TOP, 202 BOTTOM, 203 TOP, 203 BOTTOM

TIM STREET-PORTER 231, 234, 235 TOP, 235 BOTTOM

MICHAEL WESCHLER 204–5, 210 LEFT, 211 BOTTOM

COPYRIGHT © 2009 THE MONACELLI PRESS, A DIVISION OF RANDOM HOUSE, INC.

ALL RIGHTS RESERVED.

PUBLISHED IN THE UNITED STATES BY THE MONACELLI PRESS, A DIVISION OF RANDOM HOUSE, INC., NEW YORK.

THE MONACELLI PRESS AND COLOPHON ARE TRADEMARKS OF RANDOM HOUSE, INC.

LIBRARY OF CONGRESS CATALOGING-IN-PUBLICATION DATA
LUBELL, SAM.
LIVING WEST : NEW RESIDENTIAL ARCHITECTURE IN SOUTHERN CALIFORNIA/SAM LUBELL. — 1ST ED.
P. CM.
ISBN 978-1-58093-249-3 (HARDCOVER)
1. ARCHITECTURE, DOMESTIC—CALIFORNIA, SOUTHERN. 2. ARCHITECTURE—CALIFORNIA, SOUTHERN—HISTORY—21ST CENTURY.
I. TITLE. II. TITLE: NEW RESIDENTIAL ARCHITECTURE IN SOUTHERN CALIFORNIA.
NA7235.C22S685 2009
0720.9794'9090511—DC22
2009009110

PRINTED IN CHINA

DESIGN BY PS NEW YORK, PENNY HARDY, ELIZABETH OH

10 9 8 7 6 5 4 3 2 1

www.monacellipress.com